CURRY COOK

AUTHENTIC CURRY RECIPES FOR CHICKEN CURRIES, VEGETABLE CURRIES, SEAFOOD CURRIES AND MORE

By
BookSumo Press
Copyright © by Saxonberg Associates
All rights reserved

Published by
BookSumo Press, a DBA of Saxonberg Associates
http://www.booksumo.com/

ABOUT THE AUTHOR.

BookSumo Press is a publisher of unique, easy, and healthy cookbooks.

Our cookbooks span all topics and all subjects. If you want a deep dive into the possibilities of cooking with any type of ingredient. Then BookSumo Press is your go to place for robust yet simple and delicious cookbooks and recipes. Whether you are looking for great tasting pressure cooker recipes or authentic ethic and cultural food. BookSumo Press has a delicious and easy cookbook for you.

With simple ingredients, and even simpler step-by-step instructions BookSumo cookbooks get everyone in the kitchen chefing delicious meals.

BookSumo is an independent publisher of books operating in the beautiful Garden State (NJ) and our team of chefs and kitchen experts are here to teach, eat, and be merry!

INTRODUCTION

Welcome to *The Effortless Chef Series*! Thank you for taking the time to purchase this cookbook.

Come take a journey into the delights of easy cooking. The point of this cookbook and all BookSumo Press cookbooks is to exemplify the effortless nature of cooking simply.

In this book we focus on Curry. You will find that even though the recipes are simple, the taste of the dishes are quite amazing.

So will you take an adventure in simple cooking? If the answer is yes please consult the table of contents to find the dishes you are most interested in.

Once you are ready, jump right in and start cooking.

— BookSumo Press

TABLE OF CONTENTS

About the Author 2

Introduction 3

Table of Contents 4

Any Issues? Contact Us 8

Legal Notes 9

Common Abbreviations 10

Chapter 1: Easy Curry Recipes 11

    Authentic Indian Curried Pilaf 11

    Vegetarian Dream Curry 13

    Country Curried Cabbage 15

    October's Pumpkin Curried Soup 18

    Tofu Curry 101 21

    Kerala Fish Curry 24

    Jamaican Style Shrimp Curry 26

    Alternative Pumpkin Curry 29

    The Simplest Chicken Curry 32

    Anjali's Favorite 34

September's Curry Soup 37
Seafood Curry Dinner 40
South Indian Prawn Curry 42
Apple and Leeks with Potatoes Curried Soup 45
Pumpkin and Apple for Early November Curry Soup
.... 48
Beautiful Pear and Ginger Curry Soup 51
Tropical Coconut and Lime Curry Soup 54
I ♥ Curry Soup 57
Full Hanoi Curried Soup 60
Linda-Mae's Secret Curry Soup 63
Restaurant Style Shallot and Ginger Curry Soup 66
Summer Carnival Curry Soup 69
Curried Egg Soup 72
Curry Soup Combo 74
Southeast Asian Chicken Curry Soup 77
Japanese Inspired Vegetarian Tofu Curry Soup 79
North Indian Curried Cauliflower 82
Rustic Thai Mushroom Curry 85
Microwave Broccoli Curry 87

Saturday Night Curry 89

October's Apple Curry 92

Lunch Box Soup Curry 95

Whole Grain Curry 97

Vegetarian Curry Japanese Style 99

Curry Salad 103

South East Asian All Ingredient Curry 105

Punjabi Greens Curry 108

Easy Veggie Curry Soup from Vietnam 111

Vegetarian Curry Sri Lankan Style 114

Curry Paste Curry 117

Punjabi Style Curry 119

Thai Entrée Chicken Curry 122

After Work Crock Pot Orange Curry 124

Peanut Butter Coconut Curry 126

4-Ingredient Alternative Curry 128

Easy Guyanese Potato Curry 130

Jakarta Inspired Curry 132

Fruit Curry II 135

Burma Curry 137

Easy Malay Curry 140

Thursday's Night Curry and Rice 143

Canadian Inspired Curry 146

Appendix I: Spice Mixes, Curry Pastes, and Chutneys 148

Jamaican Curry Spice Mix 148

Garam Masala Spice Mix 151

Classical Indian Curry Paste 153

Simple Homemade Red Curry Paste (Thailand Style) 155

Mango Chutney I 157

Mango Chutney II 160

Curried Apricot Chutney 162

THANKS FOR READING! JOIN THE CLUB AND KEEP ON COOKING WITH 6 MORE COOKBOOKS.... 164

Come On 166

Let's Be Friends :) 166

ANY ISSUES? CONTACT US

If you find that something important to you is missing from this book please contact us at info@booksumo.com.

We will take your concerns into consideration when the 2nd edition of this book is published. And we will keep you updated!

— BookSumo Press

LEGAL NOTES

ALL RIGHTS RESERVED. NO PART OF THIS BOOK MAY BE REPRODUCED OR TRANSMITTED IN ANY FORM OR BY ANY MEANS. PHOTOCOPYING, POSTING ONLINE, AND / OR DIGITAL COPYING IS STRICTLY PROHIBITED UNLESS WRITTEN PERMISSION IS GRANTED BY THE BOOK'S PUBLISHING COMPANY. LIMITED USE OF THE BOOK'S TEXT IS PERMITTED FOR USE IN REVIEWS WRITTEN FOR THE PUBLIC.

COMMON ABBREVIATIONS

cup(s)	C.
tablespoon	tbsp
teaspoon	tsp
ounce	oz.
pound	lb

*All units used are standard American measurements

Chapter 1: Easy Curry Recipes

Authentic Indian Curried Pilaf

Ingredients

- 2 C. coconut water
- 1 C. instant rice (such as Uncle Ben's(R))
- 2 cubes chicken bouillon
- 2 tsp curry powder
- 2 pinches ground cinnamon
- 1 pinch chili powder
- 1 pinch ground turmeric
- 1 pinch ground black pepper
- 1/4 C. cashews

Directions

- In a pan, mix together the coconut water, rice, chicken bouillon, curry powder, cinnamon, chili powder, turmeric and black pepper and bring to a boil.
- Reduce the heat to low and simmer for about 6 minutes.
- Stir in the cashews and simmer for about 2 minutes.
- Remove from the heat and keep aside, covered for about 2-3 minutes.
- With a fork, fluff the rice and serve.

Amount per serving 6

Timing Information:

Preparation	10 m
Cooking	10 m
Total Time	20 m

Nutritional Information:

Calories	116 kcal
Fat	3.2 g
Carbohydrates	19.2g
Protein	3.1 g
Cholesterol	< 1 mg
Sodium	< 508 mg

* Percent Daily Values are based on a 2,000 calorie diet.

Vegetarian Dream Curry

Ingredients

- 2 C. diced butternut squash
- 1 C. water
- 1 tbsp olive oil
- 1 tsp salt
- 1/2 tsp mustard seeds
- 1/2 tsp cumin seeds
- 1/4 tsp cayenne pepper
- 1/4 tsp ground turmeric
- 1 (15 oz.) can coconut milk
- 1 (15 oz.) can cannellini beans, drained and rinsed
- 1/4 C. chopped fresh cilantro

Directions

- In a pan, add the squash, water, olive oil, salt, mustard seeds, cumin seeds, cayenne pepper and turmeric and bring to a boil.
- Reduce the heat and simmer for about 10-15 minutes, stirring occasionally.
- Stir in the coconut milk and beans and simmer for about 10 minutes.
- Serve with a garnishing of the cilantro.

Amount per serving 4

Timing Information:

Preparation	10 m
Cooking	25 m
Total Time	35 m

Nutritional Information:

Calories	397 kcal
Fat	26.7 g
Carbohydrates	34.2g
Protein	10.8 g
Cholesterol	0 mg
Sodium	607 mg

* Percent Daily Values are based on a 2,000 calorie diet.

Country Curried Cabbage

Ingredients

- 1 tbsp olive oil
- 2 tbsp butter
- 1 small yellow onion, thinly sliced
- 1 C. julienned carrots
- 1 clove garlic, minced
- 1 small head cabbage, sliced
- 1/2 C. fresh shredded coconut
- 2 tbsp Indian curry powder
- 3/4 C. coconut milk
- salt and pepper to taste
- 1/4 C. diced fresh tomato
- 1/4 C. chopped green onions
- 1/4 C. chopped cilantro

Directions

- In a large skillet, heat the oil and butter on high heat and sauté the onion, carrot and garlic for about 1 minute.
- Add the cabbage, coconut and curry powder and stir fry for about 2 minutes.
- Reduce the heat to medium-low and stir in the coconut milk, salt and pepper.
- Cook, covered till desired doneness of the curry.

- Serve with a topping of the tomato, green onions and cilantro.

Amount per serving 8

Timing Information:

Preparation	40 m
Cooking	10 m
Total Time	50 m

Nutritional Information:

Calories	140 kcal
Fat	11.1 g
Carbohydrates	10.5g
Protein	2.4 g
Cholesterol	8 mg
Sodium	127 mg

* Percent Daily Values are based on a 2,000 calorie diet.

October's Pumpkin Curried Soup

Ingredients

- 1/4 C. coconut oil
- 1 C. chopped onions
- 1 clove garlic, minced
- 3 C. vegetable broth
- 1 tsp curry powder
- 1/2 tsp salt
- 1/4 tsp ground coriander
- 1/4 tsp crushed red pepper flakes
- 1 (15 oz.) can 100% pure pumpkin
- 1 C. light coconut milk

Directions

- In a deep pan, melt the coconut oil on medium-high heat and sauté the onion for about 5 minutes.
- Stir in the vegetable broth, curry powder, salt, coriander and red pepper flakes and bring to a gentle boil.
- Boil for about 10 minutes.
- Cook, covered for about 15-20 minutes, stirring occasionally.
- Stir in the pumpkin and coconut milk and cook for about 5 minutes.
- Remove from the heat and keep aside to cool slightly.

- In a blender, add the soup in batches and pulse till smooth.
- Return the soup to pan on medium heat and cook till heated completely.

Amount per serving 6

Timing Information:

Preparation	20 m
Total Time	50 m

Nutritional Information:

Calories	171 kcal
Fat	13.5 g
Carbohydrates	12g
Protein	2 g
Cholesterol	0 mg
Sodium	601 mg

* Percent Daily Values are based on a 2,000 calorie diet.

Tofu Curry 101

Ingredients

- 4 slices fresh ginger root
- 4 cloves garlic, minced
- 1/4 C. cashews
- 2 stalks lemon grass, chopped
- 2 onions, sliced
- 3 tbsp olive oil
- 1 dash crushed red pepper flakes
- 2 tbsp curry powder
- 2 1/2 C. cubed firm tofu
- 1 (14 oz.) can coconut milk
- 14 fluid oz. water
- 2 medium potatoes, peeled and cubed
- 2 tsp salt
- 1 tbsp white sugar

Directions

- In a food processor, add the ginger root, garlic, cashews, lemon grass and onions and pulse till a paste forms.
- In a medium wok, heat the olive oil on low heat and stir in the ginger mixture and red pepper flakes.
- Slowly, add the curry powder, stirring continuously.
- Add the tofu and cook till heated completely.

- Stir in the coconut milk, water and potatoes and bring to a boil.
- Reduce the heat and simmer for about 20 minutes, stirring occasionally.
- Stir in the salt and sugar and remove from the heat.

Amount per serving 4

Timing Information:

Preparation	15 m
Cooking	30 m
Total Time	45 m

Nutritional Information:

Calories	700 kcal
Fat	49.2 g
Carbohydrates	44.9g
Protein	31.3 g
Cholesterol	0 mg
Sodium	1264 mg

* Percent Daily Values are based on a 2,000 calorie diet.

Kerala Fish Curry

Ingredients

- 1 1/2 tsp curry powder
- 1/2 tsp ground ginger
- 1/4 tsp ground turmeric
- 1/4 tsp olive oil
- 3 cloves garlic, minced
- 1 onion, chopped
- 4 1/4 oz. coconut milk, divided
- 4 1/4 oz. water, divided
- 3 1/2 oz. cod, cut into bite-size pieces
- 1 large tomato, diced

Directions

- In a skillet, add the curry powder, ground ginger and ground turmeric on medium heat and toast for about 5 minutes.
- Add the olive oil and garlic and stir to combine well.
- Add the onion and cook for about 5-7 minutes.
- Stir in the about half of the coconut milk and half of the water and simmer for about 5 minutes.
- Add the cod and simmer for about 5 minutes.
- Add the tomato, remaining coconut milk and remaining water and simmer for about 5 minutes.

Amount per serving 2

Timing Information:

Preparation	15 m
Cooking	25 m
Total Time	40 m

Nutritional Information:

Calories	237 kcal
Fat	14.2 g
Carbohydrates	18.7g
Protein	12.3 g
Cholesterol	18 mg
Sodium	51 mg

* Percent Daily Values are based on a 2,000 calorie diet.

Jamaican Style Shrimp Curry

Ingredients

- 1 tsp canola oil
- 1/2 C. minced onion
- 1/2 C. minced red bell pepper
- 1 clove garlic, minced
- 1 tsp ground cumin
- 3/4 tsp ground coriander
- 1/2 tsp curry powder
- 1/2 C. light coconut milk
- 1 tsp sugar
- 1/4 tsp crushed red pepper flakes
- 1 lb. jumbo shrimp, peeled and deveined
- 1 tbsp cornstarch
- 1 tbsp water
- 2 tbsp chopped fresh cilantro

Directions

- In a large skillet, heat the oil on medium heat and sauté the onion, red pepper and garlic for about 3 minutes.
- Stir in the cumin, coriander and curry powder and sauté for about 1 minute.
- Stir in the coconut milk, sugar and crushed red pepper flakes and bring to a boil.

- Reduce the heat and simmer, uncovered for about 2 minutes.
- Stir in the shrimp and increase the heat to medium-high.
- Cook for about 4 minutes, stirring occasionally.
- In a small bowl, dissolve the cornstarch in 1 tbsp of the water.
- Add the cornstarch mixture in the curry and stir to combine.
- Cook for about 1 minute.
- Stir in the cilantro and serve.

Amount per serving 4

Timing Information:

Preparation	10 m
Cooking	25 m
Total Time	35 m

Nutritional Information:

Calories	191 kcal
Fat	6.1 g
Carbohydrates	8.5g
Protein	24 g
Cholesterol	173 mg
Sodium	175 mg

* Percent Daily Values are based on a 2,000 calorie diet.

Alternative Pumpkin Curry

Ingredients

- 2 skinless, boneless chicken breast halves - cut into small chunks
- 1 tsp poultry seasoning
- 1 tbsp olive oil
- 1 (2 lb.) sugar pumpkin -- peeled, seeded and cubed
- 1 tbsp butter
- 1 onion, chopped
- 2 cloves garlic, chopped
- 1 (1 inch) piece fresh ginger root, finely chopped
- 1 tbsp ground coriander
- 1 tbsp ground cumin
- 1 pinch ground turmeric
- 1 tsp red pepper flakes
- 1/2 C. canned coconut milk
- 1 1/2 C. chicken broth
- salt to taste

Directions

- Season the chicken pieces with the poultry seasoning evenly.
- In a large skillet, heat the oil on medium heat and stir fry the chicken pieces till browned completely.

- Remove from the heat and keep aside.
- In another large skillet, melt the butter on medium heat and sauté the onion, garlic and ginger till the onion is translucent.
- Stir in the coriander, cumin, turmeric and red pepper flakes and sauté till fragrant.
- Add the pumpkin, cooked chicken, coconut milk, chicken broth and salt and cook for about 15-20 minutes.
- Serve this curry over the rice or noodles.

Amount per serving 4

Timing Information:

Preparation	30 m
Cooking	30 m
Total Time	1 h

Nutritional Information:

Calories	266 kcal
Fat	14.1 g
Carbohydrates	21.2g
Protein	17.5 g
Cholesterol	42 mg
Sodium	70 mg

* Percent Daily Values are based on a 2,000 calorie diet.

The Simplest Chicken Curry

Ingredients

- 2 tbsp butter
- 2 tbsp vegetable oil
- 2 sweet onions, thinly sliced
- 2 tbsp curry powder, divided
- 4 skinless, boneless chicken breast halves, cut into cubes
- 1/4 C. coconut milk
- 1/4 C. chopped peanuts

Directions

- In a large skillet, heat the oil and butter on medium heat and sauté the onions and 1 tbsp of the curry powder for about 5 minutes.
- With a slotted spoon, transfer the onions into a bowl, leaving the juice in the skillet.
- In the same skillet, add the chicken cubes and remaining 1 tbsp of the curry powder and cook for about 15 minutes, stirring occasionally.
- Add the cooked onions and coconut milk and simmer for about 15 minutes.
- Serve with a sprinkling of the chopped peanuts.

Amount per serving 4

Timing Information:

Preparation	15 m
Cooking	40 m
Total Time	55 m

Nutritional Information:

Calories	339 kcal
Fat	22.9 g
Carbohydrates	9.3g
Protein	25.5 g
Cholesterol	74 mg
Sodium	95 mg

* Percent Daily Values are based on a 2,000 calorie diet.

Anjali's Favorite

Ingredients

- 1 1/2 C. coconut milk
- 1 tbsp minced ginger
- 1 tbsp lime juice
- 1 tbsp fish sauce
- 1 tsp oyster sauce
- 2 tsp minced garlic
- 1/2 tsp chili-garlic sauce (such as Sriracha(R))
- 2 tbsp white sugar
- 1 tbsp avocado oil
- 1 lb. chicken breast, cut into bite-sized pieces
- 1/2 onion, sliced
- 1 1/2 tsp curry powder
- 2 C. broccoli florets

Directions

- In a bowl, add the coconut milk, ginger, lime juice, fish sauce, oyster sauce, garlic, chili-garlic sauce and sugar and mix till well combined.
- In a large skillet, heat the avocado oil on medium-high heat and stir fry the chicken for about 8-10 minutes.
- With a slotted spoon, transfer the chicken into a bowl and cover with a piece of the foil to keep warm.

- In the same skillet, add the onion and curry powder for about 2 minutes.
- Stir in the broccoli and stir fry for about 3 minutes.
- Add the coconut milk mixture and bring to a boil.
- Reduce the heat to medium and simmer for about 3 minutes.
- Return the chicken and cook, covered for about 3 minutes.

Amount per serving 4

Timing Information:

Preparation	15 m
Cooking	20 m
Total Time	35 m

Nutritional Information:

Calories	372 kcal
Fat	24.2 g
Carbohydrates	16g
Protein	25.8 g
Cholesterol	59 mg
Sodium	387 mg

* Percent Daily Values are based on a 2,000 calorie diet.

September's Curry Soup

Ingredients

- 1 butternut squash, halved and seeded
- 1 tbsp butter, melted
- 1 tsp salt, divided
- 3/4 tsp pumpkin pie spice, divided
- 1/4 tsp cayenne pepper
- 1 tbsp butter
- 1/2 C. chopped yellow onion
- 1 tsp yellow curry powder
- 1 (13 oz.) can coconut milk
- 2 1/2 C. vegetable stock
- 1/4 tsp freshly grated nutmeg
- 1/2 C. pepitas (pumpkin seeds)
- 1 pinch freshly grated nutmeg

Directions

- Set your oven to 425 degrees F before doing anything else.
- Arrange the butternut squash halves in a baking dish, flesh side up.
- Coat the flesh and top of the squash halves with 1 tbsp of the melted butter and sprinkle with 1/2 tsp of the salt, 1/2 tsp of the pumpkin pie spice and cayenne pepper.

- Cook in the oven for about 1 hour.
- Remove the squash from the oven and keep aside to cool for about 15 minutes.
- In a large pan, melt 1 tbsp of the butter on medium heat and sauté the onion for about 2 minutes.
- Add the curry powder and sauté for about 1 minute.
- Stir in the coconut milk and bring to a boil.
- Scoop the flesh from the butternut squash halves and add into the pan.
- Add the remaining 1/2 tsp of the salt, 1/4 tsp of the pumpkin pie spice, vegetable stock and 1/4 tsp of the nutmeg and bring to a boil.
- Reduce the heat to low and simmer till heated completely.
- With an immersion blender, blend the soup on low speed till smooth.
- Simmer for about 20 minutes.
- Season with the salt and remove from the heat.
- Serve hot with a topping of the pepitas and a pinch of nutmeg.

Amount per serving 6

Timing Information:

Preparation	15 m
Cooking	1 h 33 m
Total Time	2 h 3 m

Nutritional Information:

Calories	315 kcal
Fat	22.8 g
Carbohydrates	27.6g
Protein	6.5 g
Cholesterol	10 mg
Sodium	624 mg

* Percent Daily Values are based on a 2,000 calorie diet.

Seafood Curry Dinner

Ingredients

- 2 tbsp vegetable oil
- 1 medium onion, halved and sliced
- 1 tbsp minced fresh ginger root
- 1 tbsp minced garlic
- 1 (14 oz.) can light coconut milk
- 3 tbsp lime juice
- 1 tbsp curry paste, see appendix
- 1 tbsp brown sugar
- 12 medium shrimp, peeled (tails left on) and deveined
- 12 sea scallops, halved
- 6 oz. asparagus, cut into 2-inch pieces
- 2 tbsp chopped cilantro
- salt to taste

Directions

- In a large skillet, heat the oil on medium-high heat and sauté the onion, ginger and garlic for about 2-3 minutes.
- Stir in the coconut milk, lime juice, curry paste and brown sugar and bring to a gentle boil.
- Cook for about 5 minutes.
- Stir in the shrimp, scallops, asparagus, cilantro and salt and cook for about 5 minutes.

Amount per serving 6

Timing Information:

Preparation	20 m
Cooking	15 m
Total Time	35 m

Nutritional Information:

Calories	166 kcal
Fat	10.9 g
Carbohydrates	7.8g
Protein	8.9 g
Cholesterol	31 mg
Sodium	238 mg

* Percent Daily Values are based on a 2,000 calorie diet.

South Indian Prawn Curry

Ingredients

- 1/2 C. rice flour
- 1/2 tsp ground turmeric
- salt to taste
- 1 lb. peeled and deveined prawns
- 3 tbsp cooking oil
- 1 tsp cumin seeds
- 2 large onions, sliced thin
- 2 green chili peppers, halved lengthwise
- 1 tbsp ginger-garlic paste
- 3 C. pureed tomato
- 1/2 tsp Kashmiri red chili powder
- 1/2 tsp garam masala
- 1/2 tsp ground cumin
- 1/4 C. heavy cream (optional)
- 1/4 C. chopped fresh cilantro

Directions

- In a bowl, mix together the rice flour, turmeric and salt.
- Add the prawns and coat with the flour mixture evenly.
- In a large skillet, heat 3 tbsp of the oil on medium heat and sauté the cumin seeds till they pop.

- Add the onions, green chili peppers and ginger-garlic paste and sauté for about 5 minutes.
- Stir in the pureed tomato, Kashmiri red chili powder, garam masala, ground cumin and salt and cook for about 10-15 minutes.
- Add the cream and stir to combine.
- Add the prawns and cook for about 3-5 minutes.
- Serve with a garnishing of the cilantro.

Amount per serving 6

Timing Information:

Preparation	15 m
Cooking	30 m
Total Time	45 m

Nutritional Information:

Calories	269 kcal
Fat	11.8 g
Carbohydrates	22g
Protein	17.9 g
Cholesterol	129 mg
Sodium	166 mg

* Percent Daily Values are based on a 2,000 calorie diet.

Apple and Leeks with Potatoes Curried Soup

Ingredients

- 1 tbsp margarine
- 2 tsp curry powder
- 3 leeks, chopped
- 3/4 C. diced potatoes
- 2 Granny Smith apples -- peeled, cored and chopped
- 3 C. vegetable broth
- Salt and pepper to taste
- 1/4 C. plain yogurt

Directions

- In a medium pan, melt the butter on medium heat and sauté the curry powder for about 1 minute.
- Stir in the leeks, potato and apples and cook for about 5 minutes.
- Stir in the broth and bring to a boil.
- Reduce the heat and simmer, covered for about 20 minutes.
- Remove from the heat and keep aside to cool slightly.

- In a blender, add the soup in batches and pulse till smooth.
- Stir in the salt and pepper.
- Serve immediately with a swirl of the yogurt.

Amount per serving 4

Timing Information:

Preparation	10 m
Cooking	26 m
Total Time	36 m

Nutritional Information:

Calories	133 kcal
Fat	3.6 g
Carbohydrates	23.9g
Protein	2.9 g
Cholesterol	< 1 mg
Sodium	< 395 mg

* Percent Daily Values are based on a 2,000 calorie diet.

Pumpkin and Apple for Early November Curry Soup

Ingredients

- 4 Macintosh apples - peeled, cored and chopped
- 1 tbsp butter
- 1 onion, finely chopped
- 2 cloves garlic, crushed
- 1 tbsp curry powder
- 1 tsp ground cumin
- 1 (15 oz.) can pumpkin puree
- 4 C. chicken broth
- 1 C. water
- 1 tsp white sugar

Directions

- In a large pan, melt the butter on medium heat and sauté the onion, garlic, curry powder and cumin till the onion becomes soft.
- Stir in the apples, pumpkin, broth, water and sugar and bring to a boil, stirring occasionally.
- Reduce the heat to low and simmer, covered for about 25 minutes, stirring occasionally.

- Remove from the heat and keep aside to cool slightly.
- In a blender, add the soup in batches and pulse till smooth.
- Return the soup to pan on low heat and cook, covered till heated completely.
- Serve hot.

Amount per serving 6

Timing Information:

Preparation	20 m
Cooking	50 m
Total Time	1 h 10 m

Nutritional Information:

Calories	131 kcal
Fat	3.4 g
Carbohydrates	22.6g
Protein	4.7 g
Cholesterol	5 mg
Sodium	696 mg

* Percent Daily Values are based on a 2,000 calorie diet.

Beautiful Pear and Ginger Curry Soup

Ingredients

- 1 (2 lb.) butternut squash
- 3 tbsp unsalted butter
- 1 onion, diced
- 2 cloves garlic, minced
- 2 tsp minced fresh ginger root
- 1 tbsp curry powder
- 1 tsp salt
- 4 C. reduced sodium chicken broth
- 2 firm ripe Bartlett pears, peeled, cored, and cut into 1 inch dice
- 1/2 C. half and half

Directions

- Set your oven to 450 degrees F before doing anything else and line a rimmed baking sheet with a parchment paper.
- Cut the squash in half lengthwise.
- Remove the seeds and membrane.
- Arrange the squash halves onto the prepared baking sheet, cut sides down.

- Cook in the oven for about 45 minutes.
- Remove from the oven and scoop the flesh from the squash halves.
- In a large pan, melt the butter on medium heat and sauté the onion, garlic, ginger, curry powder and salt for about 10 minutes.
- Add the chicken broth and bring to a boil.
- Stir in the pears and squash flesh and simmer for about 30 minutes.
- Remove from the heat and keep aside to cool slightly.
- In a blender, add the soup in batches and pulse till smooth.
- Return the soup to the pan and stir in the half and half.
- Cook till heated completely.
- Serve hot.

Amount per serving 8

Timing Information:

Preparation	15 m
Cooking	1 h 30 m
Total Time	1 h 45 m

Nutritional Information:

Calories	167 kcal
Fat	6.6 g
Carbohydrates	27.5g
Protein	3 g
Cholesterol	20 mg
Sodium	786 mg

* Percent Daily Values are based on a 2,000 calorie diet.

Tropical Coconut and Lime Curry Soup

Ingredients

- 6 carrots, peeled and chopped
- 1/2 head cauliflower, trimmed and chopped
- 1 1/2 tsp olive oil
- 2 cloves garlic, chopped
- 1 tsp salt
- 1 tsp ground black pepper
- 3 C. vegetable broth
- 1 tbsp curry powder
- 1 C. coconut milk
- 1/2 lime, juiced

Directions

- Set your oven to 400 degrees F before doing anything else.
- In a casserole dish, add the carrots, cauliflower, olive oil, garlic, salt and black pepper and toss to coat well.
- Cook in the oven for about 45 minutes, stirring once after 20 minutes.
- Remove from the oven and stir well.

- In a large pan, add the vegetable broth and bring to a boil.
- Stir in the curry powder and roasted vegetables and bring to a boil.
- Cook, covered for about 8-10 minutes.
- Remove from the heat.
- With an immersion blender, blend the soup till smooth.
- Return the pan on medium heat.
- Stir in the coconut milk and lime juice and simmer for about 5-10 minutes.
- Serve hot.

Amount per serving 6

Timing Information:

Preparation	10 m
Cooking	1 h
Total Time	1 h 10 m

Nutritional Information:

Calories	143 kcal
Fat	9.8 g
Carbohydrates	13.4g
Protein	3 g
Cholesterol	0 mg
Sodium	680 mg

* Percent Daily Values are based on a 2,000 calorie diet.

I ♥ Curry Soup

Ingredients

- 1 butternut squash, halved and seeded
- 1 tbsp butter, melted
- 1 tsp salt, divided
- 3/4 tsp pumpkin pie spice, divided
- 1/4 tsp cayenne pepper
- 1 tbsp butter
- 1/2 C. chopped yellow onion
- 1 tsp yellow curry powder
- 1 (13 oz.) can coconut milk
- 2 1/2 C. vegetable stock
- 1/4 tsp freshly grated nutmeg
- 1/2 C. pepitas (pumpkin seeds)
- 1 pinch freshly grated nutmeg

Directions

- Set your oven to 425 degrees F before doing anything else.
- Arrange the butternut squash in a baking dish, flesh side up.

- Coat the flesh of squash with 1 tbsp of the melted butter and sprinkle with 1/2 tsp of the salt, 1/2 tsp of the pumpkin pie spice and cayenne pepper.
- Cook in the oven for about 1 hour.
- Remove the squash from the oven and keep aside to cool for about 15 minutes.
- Scoop flesh from the butternut squash.
- In a large pan, melt 1 tbsp of the butter on medium heat and sauté the onion for about 2 minutes.
- Add the curry powder and sauté for about 1 minute.
- Stir in the coconut milk and bring to a boil.
- Add the squash flesh, remaining 1/2 tsp of the salt, 1/4 tsp pumpkin pie spice, vegetable stock, and 1/4 tsp of the nutmeg and bring to a boil.
- Reduce the heat to low and simmer till heated completely.
- With an immersion blender, blend the soup on low speed till smooth.
- Simmer for about 20 minutes.
- Stir in the salt and remove from the heat.
- Serve hot with a topping of the pepitas and a pinch of nutmeg.

Amount per serving 6

Timing Information:

Preparation	15 m
Cooking	1 h 33 m
Total Time	2 h 3 m

Nutritional Information:

Calories	315 kcal
Fat	22.8 g
Carbohydrates	27.6g
Protein	6.5 g
Cholesterol	10 mg
Sodium	624 mg

* Percent Daily Values are based on a 2,000 calorie diet.

Full Hanoi Curried Soup

Ingredients

- 2 tbsp vegetable oil
- 1 (3 lb.) whole chicken, skin removed and cut into pieces
- 1 onion, cut into chunks
- 2 shallots, thinly sliced
- 2 cloves garlic, chopped
- 1/8 C. thinly sliced fresh ginger root
- 1 stalk lemon grass, cut into 2 inch pieces
- 4 tbsp curry powder
- 1 green bell pepper, cut into 1 inch pieces
- 2 carrots, sliced diagonally
- 1 quart chicken broth
- 1 quart water
- 2 tbsp fish sauce
- 2 kaffir lime leaves
- 1 bay leaf
- 2 tsp red pepper flakes
- 8 small potatoes, quartered
- 1 (14 oz.) can coconut milk
- 1 bunch fresh cilantro

Directions

- In a large pan, heat the oil on medium heat and cook the chicken and onion till the onion becomes translucent.
- Transfer the chicken mixture into a bowl and keep aside.
- In the same pan, add the shallots and sauté for about 1 minute.
- Stir in the garlic, ginger, lemon grass and curry powder and cook for about 5 minutes.
- Stir in the bell peppers, carrots, chicken mixture, chicken broth, water, fish sauce, lime leaves, bay leaf and red pepper flakes and bring to a boil.
- Stir in the potatoes and again bring to a boil.
- Stir in the coconut milk.
- Reduce the heat and simmer for about 40-60 minutes.
- Serve with a garnishing of the fresh cilantro sprigs.

Amount per serving 8

Timing Information:

Preparation	30 m
Cooking	2 h
Total Time	2 h 30 m

Nutritional Information:

Calories	512 kcal
Fat	26.8 g
Carbohydrates	40.6g
Protein	29.8 g
Cholesterol	75 mg
Sodium	374 mg

* Percent Daily Values are based on a 2,000 calorie diet.

Curry Cookbook

Linda-Mae's Secret Curry Soup

Ingredients

- 1 butternut squash
- 1 tbsp olive oil
- 1 onion, chopped
- 1 shallot, minced
- 2 tbsp curry powder
- 1 tsp ground turmeric
- 1 apple, cored and chopped
- 1 slice fresh ginger, minced
- Water to cover
- 1 (14 oz.) can coconut milk
- Salt to taste

Directions

- Set your oven to 350 degrees F before doing anything else.
- With a fork, pierce the butternut squash and arrange onto a baking sheet.
- Cook in the oven for about 45 minutes.
- Remove from the oven and keep aside to cool slightly.
- Cut the squash in half.
- Peel, scoop the seeds and chop the flesh.

- In a skillet, heat the olive oil on medium heat and sauté the onion and shallot for about 10 minutes.
- Add the curry powder and turmeric and sauté for about 2 minutes.
- Stir in the squash, apple, ginger and enough water to cover and bring to a boil.
- Reduce the heat to medium-low and simmer for about 15 minutes.
- With an immersion blender, blend till the squash is broken into pieces.
- Stir in the coconut milk and salt and simmer for about 3 minutes.

Amount per serving 4

Timing Information:

Preparation	15 m
Cooking	1 h 20 m
Total Time	1 h 45 m

Nutritional Information:

Calories	388 kcal
Fat	25.1 g
Carbohydrates	44.3g
Protein	5.7 g
Cholesterol	0 mg
Sodium	68 mg

* Percent Daily Values are based on a 2,000 calorie diet.

Restaurant Style Shallot and Ginger Curry Soup

Ingredients

- 2 tsp canola oil
- 1/2 C. chopped shallots
- 3 C. 1/2-inch cubes peeled sweet potato
- 1 1/2 C. 1/4-inch slices peeled carrot
- 1 tbsp grated fresh ginger root
- 2 tsp curry powder
- 3 C. fat free, low-sodium chicken broth
- 1/2 tsp salt

Directions

- In a large pan, heat the oil on medium-high heat and sauté the shallots for about 3 minutes.
- Stir in the sweet potato, carrot, ginger and curry powder and sauté for about 3-4 minutes.
- Add the chicken broth and bring to a boil.
- Reduce the heat to low and simmer, covered for about 25-30 minutes.
- Stir in the salt.
- Remove from the heat and keep aside to cool slightly.

- In a blender, add the soup in batches and pulse till smooth.
- Serve immediately.

Amount per serving 5

Timing Information:

Preparation	15 m
Cooking	35 m
Total Time	50 m

Nutritional Information:

Calories	131 kcal
Fat	2.1 g
Carbohydrates	23.1g
Protein	5.7 g
Cholesterol	0 mg
Sodium	539 mg

* Percent Daily Values are based on a 2,000 calorie diet.

Summer Carnival Curry Soup

Ingredients

- 2 tbsp olive oil
- 1 1/2 tbsp mild curry paste, see appendix
- 1 small red onion, chopped
- 1 carrot, chopped
- 1 celery stalk, chopped
- 1 small red bell pepper, chopped
- 1/2 tsp red pepper flakes
- 2 cubes vegetable bouillon
- 1/2 lb. lentils
- 3 C. water, more if needed
- 3/4 C. spaghetti sauce
- 1/2 C. chopped fresh cilantro
- 1 pinch ground black pepper to taste

Directions

- In a large pan, heat the oil on medium heat and sauté the onion, carrot, celery, red bell pepper, and red pepper flakes for about 5-10 minutes.
- Break the bouillon cubes into onion mixture.
- Add the lentils and stir to combine well.

- Add enough water into the pot, that is 1-inch above the lentil mixture and bring to a boil.
- Reduce the heat to low and simmer for about 40 minutes.
- Stir in the spaghetti sauce and simmer for about 5 minutes.
- Stir in the cilantro and black pepper and serve.

Amount per serving 4

Timing Information:

Preparation	15 m
Cooking	50 m
Total Time	1 h 5 m

Nutritional Information:

Calories	339 kcal
Fat	9 g
Carbohydrates	48.4g
Protein	16.7 g
Cholesterol	< 1 mg
Sodium	< 389 mg

* Percent Daily Values are based on a 2,000 calorie diet.

Curried Egg Soup

Ingredients

- 1/2 C. chicken broth
- 1/2 C. coconut milk
- 1 green onion, chopped
- 1 tbsp chopped fresh cilantro
- 1/8 tsp curry powder
- 1/8 tsp chili powder
- 1 pinch ground ginger
- 1 egg, beaten

Directions

- In a pan, add the chicken broth, coconut milk, green onion, cilantro, curry powder, chili powder and ground ginger and bring to a boil.
- Reduce the heat and simmer.
- Slowly, drizzle the beaten egg, beating continuously.
- Cook for about 23 minutes.
- Serve hot.

Amount per serving 1

Timing Information:

Preparation	10 m
Cooking	10 m
Total Time	20 m

Nutritional Information:

Calories	312 kcal
Fat	29.5 g
Carbohydrates	6.3g
Protein	9.6 g
Cholesterol	188 mg
Sodium	572 mg

* Percent Daily Values are based on a 2,000 calorie diet.

Curry Soup Combo

Ingredients

- 2 quarts chicken stock
- 1 (8.4 oz.) package yellow curry sauce
- 8 oz. cubed cooked chicken
- 1 C. sliced fresh mushrooms
- 2 stalks lemon grass, trimmed and chopped
- 2 cloves garlic, minced
- 1 (14 oz.) can coconut cream
- 1 (16 oz.) package large dried Thai-style rice noodles

Directions

- In a pan, add the chicken stock and bring to a boil.
- Add the curry sauce and stir to combine well.
- Reduce the heat to medium and stir in the chicken, mushrooms, lemon grass and garlic and stir to combine.
- Bring to a simmer and cook for about 30 minutes.
- Reduce the heat to medium-low and stir in the coconut cream.
- Discard the lemon grass.
- In a large bowl, soak the noodles in hot water for about 15 minutes.
- Drain and rinse the noodles completely.

- In a large pan of boiling water, cook the rice noodles for about 8 minutes.
- Drain the noodles.
- Divide the noodles into serving bowls and top with the soup.
- Serve immediately.

Amount per serving 6

Timing Information:

Preparation	10 m
Cooking	45 m
Total Time	55 m

Nutritional Information:

Calories	624 kcal
Fat	16.7 g
Carbohydrates	101.8g
Protein	15.8 g
Cholesterol	29 mg
Sodium	1227 mg

* Percent Daily Values are based on a 2,000 calorie diet.

Southeast Asian Chicken Curry Soup

Ingredients

- 1 (14 oz.) can coconut milk
- 2 tsp green curry paste, see appendix
- 2 tsp lime juice
- 1/4 tsp salt, or to taste
- 1/8 tsp ground white pepper
- 1 dash hot sauce
- 1 pinch ground cumin
- 1 1/2 C. cubed cooked chicken
- 1 (10 oz.) can mushroom stems and pieces, undrained
- 1 green onion, chopped, divided

Directions

- In a pan, add the coconut milk on medium heat and cook for about 5 minutes.
- Add the green curry paste, lime juice, salt, pepper, hot sauce and cumin and beat till well combined.
- Stir in the chicken, mushrooms and white part of the green onion and simmer for about 5-10 minutes.
- Serve with a garnishing of the remaining green onion.

Amount per serving 2

Timing Information:

Preparation	10 m
Cooking	10 m
Total Time	20 m

Nutritional Information:

Calories	661 kcal
Fat	58.4 g
Carbohydrates	14.9g
Protein	34.6 g
Cholesterol	82 mg
Sodium	1100 mg

* Percent Daily Values are based on a 2,000 calorie diet.

Japanese Inspired Vegetarian Tofu Curry Soup

Ingredients

- 1 tbsp olive oil
- 1 onion, finely chopped
- 2 cloves garlic, minced
- 1/4 C. water
- 2 carrots, chopped
- 1/2 zucchini, chopped
- 1 1/2 tbsp ground coriander
- 1 1/2 tbsp ground cumin
- 2 1/2 tsp ground turmeric
- 2 1/2 tsp ground ginger
- 1 tbsp curry powder
- 1 (16 oz.) package extra-firm tofu, drained and cubed
- 1 quart vegetable broth
- 1/2 (16 oz.) package uncooked whole wheat spaghetti
- 1 (5 oz.) can nonfat evaporated milk
- 2 tbsp coconut extract
- Salt and pepper to taste

Directions

- In a large skillet, heat the oil on medium heat and sauté the onion and garlic till tender.
- Stir in the water, carrots, zucchini, coriander, cumin, turmeric, ginger, curry powder and tofu and cook for about 10 minutes.
- In a large pan, add the broth and bring to boil.
- Add the noodles and cook for about 3 minutes.
- Stir in the tofu mixture with the evaporated milk, coconut extract, salt and pepper and cook till noodles become soft.

Amount per serving 4

Timing Information:

Preparation	15 m
Cooking	20 m
Total Time	35 m

Nutritional Information:

Calories	430 kcal
Fat	12.7 g
Carbohydrates	57.9g
Protein	24.1 g
Cholesterol	1 mg
Sodium	< 524 mg

* Percent Daily Values are based on a 2,000 calorie diet.

NORTH INDIAN CURRIED CAULIFLOWER

Ingredients

- 2 tbsp unsweetened coconut cream
- 5 tbsp milk
- 1 tbsp tamarind pulp
- 2 tbsp boiling water
- 1 tbsp chickpea flour
- 1/2 tsp chili powder
- 1 tsp coriander seed
- 1 head cauliflower, broken into small florets
- 1 tsp mustard seed
- 2 tbsp vegetable oil for frying
- salt to taste

Directions

- In a bowl, dissolve the coconut cream in 5 tbsp of the milk.
- In another bowl, soak the tamarind in 2 tbsp of the boiling water for about 5-10 minutes.
- Squeeze the husk and discard the tamarind piece, reserving the water.
- In a bowl, add the tamarind water, flour, chili powder and coriander and mix till well combined.
- Add the cauliflower and coconut milk and stir to coat well.

- In a pan, heat the oil and sauté the mustard seeds till they start to pop.
- Add the cauliflower mixture and simmer, covered till the cauliflower becomes tender, stirring occasionally.

Amount per serving (4 total)

Timing Information:

Preparation	5 m
Cooking	10 m
Total Time	15 m

Nutritional Information:

Calories	95 kcal
Fat	4.1 g
Carbohydrates	12.9g
Protein	4.4 g
Cholesterol	2 mg
Sodium	56 mg

* Percent Daily Values are based on a 2,000 calorie diet.

Rustic Thai Mushroom Curry

Ingredients

- 2 C. coconut milk
- 1 (2 inch) piece galangal, peeled and sliced
- 3 kaffir lime leaves, torn
- 2 tsp salt
- 1/3 lb. sliced fresh mushrooms
- 5 Thai chili peppers, chopped
- 1/4 C. fresh lime juice
- 1 tbsp fish sauce

Directions

- In a pan, add the coconut milk and galangal and bring to a boil.
- Add the kaffir lime leaves and salt and simmer for about 10 minutes.
- Add the mushrooms and cook for about 5-7 minutes.
- Remove from the heat and stir in the lime juice and fish sauce.
- Serve with a topping of the Thai chilies.

Amount per serving (4 total)

Timing Information:

Preparation	10 m
Cooking	20 m
Total Time	30 m

Nutritional Information:

Calories	261 kcal
Fat	24.4 g
Carbohydrates	11.8g
Protein	4.9 g
Cholesterol	0 mg
Sodium	1458 mg

* Percent Daily Values are based on a 2,000 calorie diet.

Microwave Broccoli Curry

Ingredients

- 1 onion, sliced
- 2 tbsp red curry paste
- 3 C. broccoli, sliced
- 1 (400 g) can chickpeas, drained
- 1 C. light coconut milk
- 1 tbsp lemon juice
- 1 tbsp soy sauce
- 1/2 C. nuts, chopped

Directions

- In a large microwave safe casserole dish, place the onion and curry paste and cook on Very High for about 2 minutes.
- Add the broccoli, chick peas, coconut milk, lemon juice and soy sauce and cook on Very High for about 6-8 minutes.
- Serve over the jasmine rice with a garnishing of the nuts.

Servings per Recipe: 4

Timing Information:

Total Time	25mins
Prep Time	15 MINS
Cook Time	10 MINS

Nutritional Information:

Calories	235.9
Fat	10 g
Cholesterol	0 mg
Sodium	665.8 mg
Carbohydrates	30.3 g
Protein	8.7 g

* Percent Daily Values are based on a 2,000 calorie diet.

Saturday Night Curry

Ingredients

- 2 bunches green onions
- 1 (14 oz.) can light coconut milk
- 1/4 C. soy sauce, divided
- 1/2 tsp brown sugar
- 1 1/2 tsp curry powder
- 1 tsp minced fresh ginger
- 2 tsp chili paste
- 1 lb. firm tofu, cut into 3/4 inch cubes
- 4 roma (plum) tomatoes, chopped
- 1 yellow bell pepper, thinly sliced
- 4 oz. fresh mushrooms, chopped
- 1/4 C. chopped fresh basil
- 4 C. chopped bok choy
- salt to taste

Directions

- Chop the white parts of the green onions finely.
- Chop the green parts of the green onions into 2-inch pieces.
- In a large heavy skillet, mix together the coconut milk, 3 tbsp of the soy sauce, brown sugar, curry powder, ginger and chili paste and bring to a boil.

- Stir in the tofu, tomatoes, yellow pepper, mushrooms and white part of the green onions and cook, covered for about 5 minutes, stirring occasionally.
- Stir in the basil, bok choy, salt and remaining soy sauce and cook for about 5 minutes.
- Serve with a garnishing of the green parts of the green onion.

Amount per serving (6 total)

Timing Information:

Preparation	25 m
Cooking	15 m
Total Time	40 m

Nutritional Information:

Calories	232 kcal
Fat	13.2 g
Carbohydrates	16.9g
Protein	16.5 g
Cholesterol	0 mg
Sodium	680 mg

* Percent Daily Values are based on a 2,000 calorie diet.

October's Apple Curry

Ingredients

- 1 C. red lentils
- 1 C. brown lentils
- 8 C. water
- 1/2 tsp turmeric
- 1 tbsp canola oil
- 1 large onion, diced
- 2 tomatoes, cored and chopped
- 3 cloves garlic, minced
- 1 1/2 tbsp curry powder
- 2 tsp ground cumin
- 1/2 tsp salt
- 1/2 tsp black pepper
- 1/4 tsp ground cloves
- 2 C. peeled, cubed (1-inch), seeded pumpkin
- 2 potatoes, unpeeled and chopped
- 2 carrots, peeled and diced
- 2 C. packed fresh spinach, chopped
- 1 Granny Smith apple, unpeeled, cored and diced

Directions

- In a pan, add the both lentils, water and turmeric on medium-low heat and cook for about 45 minutes.
- Drain well, reserving 2 1/2 C. of the cooking liquid.
- Meanwhile in a large deep pan, heat the canola oil on medium heat and sauté the onion for about 5 minutes.
- Stir in the tomatoes and garlic and cook for about 5 minutes, stirring occasionally.
- Stir in the curry powder, cumin, salt, pepper and cloves.
- Increase the heat to medium-low and stir in the cooked lentil, reserved cooking liquid, pumpkin, potatoes and carrots and simmer, covered for about 35-45 minutes.
- Stir in the spinach and apple and simmer for about 15 minutes.

Amount per serving (6 total)

Timing Information:

Preparation	30 m
Cooking	1 h 40 m
Total Time	2 h 10 m

Nutritional Information:

Calories	360 kcal
Fat	3.7 g
Carbohydrates	64.3g
Protein	20.1 g
Cholesterol	0 mg
Sodium	244 mg

* Percent Daily Values are based on a 2,000 calorie diet.

Lunch Box Soup Curry

Ingredients

- 2 tbsp vegetable oil
- 1 onion, chopped
- 1 tbsp curry powder
- 2 lb. carrots, chopped
- 4 C. vegetable broth
- 2 C. water

Directions

- In a large pan, heat the oil on medium heat and sauté the onion till tender.
- Stir in the curry powder.
- Add the chopped carrots and stir to combine well.
- Add the vegetable broth and simmer for about 20 minutes.
- Remove from the heat and keep aside to cool slightly.
- Transfer the soup mixture into a blender and pulse till smooth.
- Return the soup in the pan and, add enough water to thin according to your required consistency.
- Cook till heated completely before serving.

Amount per serving (6 total)

Timing Information:

Preparation	15 m
Cooking	25 m
Total Time	40 m

Nutritional Information:

Calories	133 kcal
Fat	5.4 g
Carbohydrates	20.2g
Protein	2.4 g
Cholesterol	0 mg
Sodium	415 mg

* Percent Daily Values are based on a 2,000 calorie diet.

Whole Grain Curry

Ingredients

- 1 C. millet
- 2 tbsp olive oil
- 1 onion, diced
- 2 cloves garlic, diced
- 2 1/2 C. water
- 1 tsp salt
- 1/2 tsp ground cumin
- 2 tsp curry powder

Directions

- In a large bowl of the water, soak the millet for about 8 hours to overnight.
- Drain the millet completely.
- In a large skillet, heat the oil on medium heat and sauté the onion and garlic for about 10-15 minutes.
- Stir in the millet, 2 1/2 C. of the water, salt and cumin and simmer, covered for about 20 minutes.
- Stir in the curry powder and remove from the heat.

Amount per serving (4 total)

Timing Information:

Preparation	10 m
Cooking	30 m
Total Time	8 h 40 m

Nutritional Information:

Calories	278 kcal
Fat	9.1 g
Carbohydrates	42.9g
Protein	6.4 g
Cholesterol	0 mg
Sodium	592 mg

* Percent Daily Values are based on a 2,000 calorie diet.

Vegetarian Curry Japanese Style

Ingredients

- 2 C. cubed Japanese turnips
- 1 potato, peeled and cubed
- 1 tomato, diced
- 1 C. water
- 1/4 tsp ground turmeric
- Spice Paste:
- 1 tsp canola oil
- 2 dried red chilis
- 2 small Thai green chilis
- 1 (1/2 inch) piece cinnamon stick
- 4 pearl onions
- 2 tbsp unsweetened dried coconut
- 1 tbsp coriander seeds
- 5 cashews
- 2 green cardamom pods
- 2 whole cloves
- 1/2 tsp fennel seeds
- 1/4 tsp cumin seeds
- 2 tbsp chopped cilantro
- 2 tbsp chopped fresh mint
- 1 tsp water, or as needed
- 1 tsp canola oil
- 1/2 tsp fennel seeds

- 1 (1 inch) piece cinnamon stick
- 2 cloves garlic, minced
- 1 (1 inch) piece fresh ginger root, minced
- 4 fresh curry leaves
- 1/4 C. peas
- 1 pinch salt

Directions

- In a large pan, add the turnips, potato, diced tomato, 1 C. of the water and turmeric and bring to a boil.
- Reduce the heat and simmer for about 15 minutes.
- In a skillet, heat 1 tsp of the canola oil on medium heat and sauté the chilis, 1/2-inch piece of the cinnamon stick, pearl onions, coconut, coriander, cashews, cardamom pods, cloves, 1/2 tsp of the fennel seeds and cumin seeds for about 3 minutes.
- Remove from the heat and transfer into a spice grinder.
- Add the cilantro, mint and 1 tsp of the water and grind till a smooth paste forms.
- In a large skillet, heat 1 tsp of the canola oil on medium-low heat and sauté 1/2 tsp of the fennel seeds and 1-inch piece of the cinnamon stick for about 30 seconds.
- Add the minced garlic, ginger and curry leaves and sauté for about 2 minutes.
- Add the cooked vegetables and spice paste and bring to a boil. (Add more water if curry becomes too thick.)
- Stir in the green peas and salt.

- Reduce the heat and simmer for about 10 minutes.

Amount per serving (2 total)

Timing Information:

Preparation	30 m
Cooking	30 m
Total Time	1 h

Nutritional Information:

Calories	297 kcal
Fat	11.6 g
Carbohydrates	45.1g
Protein	8 g
Cholesterol	0 mg
Sodium	236 mg

* Percent Daily Values are based on a 2,000 calorie diet.

Curry Salad

Ingredients

- 1 sweet apple, grated
- 2 carrots, grated
- 1/4 C. raisins
- 2 tbsp chopped fresh parsley
- Dressing:
- 1 lemon, juiced
- 2 tbsp olive oil
- 1 tbsp toasted sesame seeds
- 1 tsp curry powder
- 1/2 tsp maple syrup
- salt and ground black pepper to taste

Directions

- In a large bowl, mix together the apple, carrots, raisins and parsley.
- In a container with a tight-fitting lid, mix together the remaining ingredients.
- Cover the jar tightly and shake till well combined.
- Place the dressing over the salad and mix till well combined.

Amount per serving (2 total)

Timing Information:

Preparation	
Cooking	20 m
Total Time	20 m

Nutritional Information:

Calories	292 kcal
Fat	16.3 g
Carbohydrates	40.4g
Protein	3 g
Cholesterol	0 mg
Sodium	127 mg

* Percent Daily Values are based on a 2,000 calorie diet.

South East Asian All Ingredient Curry

Ingredients

Brown Rice:

- 3 C. water
- 2 C. brown rice
- 1 tbsp soy sauce
- 1/2 tsp salt

Panang Curry:

- 1 tbsp vegetable oil
- 2 1/2 tbsp red curry paste
- 1 (14 oz.) can coconut milk
- 1 tbsp vegetarian fish sauce
- 1 tbsp white sugar
- 5 kaffir lime leaves
- 8 oz. fried tofu, cubed
- 2 C. broccoli florets
- 1/2 red bell pepper, chopped into 1-inch pieces
- 1/4 C. diagonally sliced carrots

Directions

- In a rice cooker, mix together the water, brown rice, soy sauce and salt.
- Cook, covered about 35 minutes according to manufacturer's directions.
- In a wide skillet, heat the vegetable oil on medium heat and sauté the curry paste for about 1-2 minutes.
- Add the coconut milk, fish sauce, white sugar and lime leaves and stir to combine.
- Reduce the heat to medium-low and simmer, covered for about 5 minutes.
- Stir in the tofu, broccoli, red bell pepper and carrots and simmer for about 1-2 minutes.
- Serve this curry over the cooked brown rice.

Amount per serving (4 total)

Timing Information:

Preparation	20 m
Cooking	42 m
Total Time	1 h 2 m

Nutritional Information:

Calories	765 kcal
Fat	38.5 g
Carbohydrates	90.6g
Protein	20.6 g
Cholesterol	0 mg
Sodium	749 mg

* Percent Daily Values are based on a 2,000 calorie diet.

Punjabi Greens Curry

Ingredients

- 2 tbsp vegetable oil, divided
- 2 C. chopped fresh spinach
- 1 tsp ground cumin
- 3/4 C. chopped onion
- 2 green chili peppers, chopped
- 2 tsp chopped garlic
- 2 tomatoes, chopped
- 1/2 C. water
- 2 tsp ground coriander
- 1 tsp ground red chilis
- 2 tbsp salt
- 8 oz. paneer, cubed

Directions

- In a skillet, heat 1 tbsp of the vegetable oil on medium heat and cook the spinach for about 3-4 minutes.
- Remove from the heat and keep aside to cool slightly.
- Transfer the spinach into a food processor and pulse till a rough paste forms.
- In a pan, heat the remaining 1 tbsp of the oil on medium heat and sauté the cumin for about 30 seconds.

- Add the onion, green chili peppers and garlic and sauté for about 3-4 minutes.
- Stir in the tomatoes and simmer, covered for about 1 minute.
- Add the spinach paste, water, ground coriander, red chili powder and salt and cook for about 2-3 minutes.
- Stir in the paneer and simmer for about 1-2 minutes more.

Amount per serving (2 total)

Timing Information:

Preparation	15 m
Cooking	20 m
Total Time	35 m

Nutritional Information:

Calories	333 kcal
Fat	20.1 g
Carbohydrates	22.7g
Protein	18.9 g
Cholesterol	17 mg
Sodium	7499 mg

* Percent Daily Values are based on a 2,000 calorie diet.

Easy Veggie Curry Soup from Vietnam

Ingredients

- 1/2 onion, diced
- 2 1/2 tbsp curry powder
- 1 (32 fluid oz.) container chicken broth
- 1/2 lemon, sliced
- 1 1/4-inch-thick slices fresh ginger, peeled
- 1 1/2 tsp white sugar
- salt to taste
- 1 lb. assorted mushrooms
- 1 (13.5 oz.) can coconut milk
- 1 tbsp fresh lemon juice
- salt to taste
- 8 kaffir lime leaves

Directions

- Heat a greased pan on high heat and sauté the onion for about 2 minutes.
- Stir in the curry powder.
- Add the chicken broth, lemon, ginger, sugar and salt and stir to combine.

- Reduce the heat to medium and cook for about 2-3 minutes.
- Stir in the mushrooms and cook for about 3 minutes.
- Stir in in the coconut milk and lemon juice and remove from the heat.
- Stir in the lime leaves and keep aside for about 5 minutes.
- Discard the lime leaves before serving.

Amount per serving (4 total)

Timing Information:

Preparation	20 m
Cooking	12 m
Total Time	37 m

Nutritional Information:

Calories	264 kcal
Fat	22.1 g
Carbohydrates	16.4g
Protein	6.1 g
Cholesterol	6 mg
Sodium	1331 mg

* Percent Daily Values are based on a 2,000 calorie diet.

Vegetarian Curry Sri Lankan Style

Ingredients

- 3/4 tsp coriander seed
- 1/4 tsp fennel seed
- 1/4 tsp cumin seed
- 4 leaves fresh curry
- 4 large potatoes - peeled and cubed
- 1 tbsp ghee (clarified butter)
- 1/2 onion, finely chopped
- 1 clove garlic, minced
- 1 (1 inch) piece fresh ginger root, grated
- 1/2 tsp cumin seed
- 1/2 tsp coriander seed
- 1/2 C. coconut milk
- 1 tbsp chopped fresh cilantro
- salt to taste

Directions

- For the fresh curry powder, in a small skillet, dry roast the 3/4 tsp of the coriander, 1/4 tsp of the fennel, and 1/4 tsp of the cumin seeds individually till aromatic.

- In the same skillet, mix together all the roasted spices and curry leaves on low heat and dry roast for about 5 minutes more.
- With a mortar and pestle, grind the spices and curry leaves.
- Now, with the mortar and pestle, grind the remaining coriander and cumin seeds.
- In a microwave safe bowl, place the potato cubes and microwave for about 3-5 minutes.
- In a large skillet, melt the ghee on medium heat and sauté the onion, garlic and ginger till golden and aromatic.
- Add the cumin and coriander seeds powder and fresh curry powder and sauté for about 30 seconds.
- Stir in the potatoes and cook for about 3 minutes.
- Stir in the coconut milk and bring to a gentle boil.
- Reduce the heat to low and simmer, covered for about 7 minutes.
- Stir in the salt and remove from the heat.
- Serve with a topping of the chopped fresh cilantro.

Amount per serving (4 total)

Timing Information:

Preparation	20 m
Cooking	15 m
Total Time	35 m

Nutritional Information:

Calories	381 kcal
Fat	9.8 g
Carbohydrates	67.9g
Protein	8.6 g
Cholesterol	8 mg
Sodium	609 mg

* Percent Daily Values are based on a 2,000 calorie diet.

Curry Paste Curry

Ingredients

- 5 tbsp curry paste, see appendix
- cooking oil
- 4 C. coconut milk
- 2/3 lb. skinless, boneless chicken breast, cubed
- 2 tbsp palm sugar
- 2 tbsp fish sauce
- 6 kaffir lime leaves, torn
- 2 fresh red chili peppers, sliced
- 1/4 C. fresh Thai basil leaves

Directions

- In a large skillet, heat the oil on medium heat and sauté the curry paste till fragrant.
- Stir in the coconut milk and bring to a boil.
- Stir in the chicken and cook for about 10-15 minutes.
- Stir the palm sugar, fish sauce, and lime leaves and simmer for about 5 minutes.
- Serve with a garnishing of the sliced red chili peppers and Thai basil leaves.

Amount per serving (4 total)

Timing Information:

Preparation	15 m
Cooking	20 m
Total Time	35 m

Nutritional Information:

Calories	596 kcal
Fat	51.2 g
Carbohydrates	18.5g
Protein	22.3 g
Cholesterol	46 mg
Sodium	981 mg

* Percent Daily Values are based on a 2,000 calorie diet.

PUNJABI STYLE CURRY

Ingredients

- 1/4 C. plain yogurt
- 2 tsp garam masala
- 2 tsp paprika
- 1/2 tsp freshly ground black pepper
- 1/2 tsp salt
- 1/2 tsp cayenne pepper
- 1/2 tsp ground coriander
- 1 lb. skinless, boneless chicken breast - cut into 1-inch strips
- 3 tbsp vegetable oil
- 1 tsp cumin seeds
- 1 large onion, chopped
- 3 cloves garlic, minced
- 1 tbsp grated fresh ginger
- 2 green chili peppers, minced
- 2 Roma tomatoes, diced
- 1/2 C. tomato paste
- 1/4 C. water
- 1 tsp garam masala
- 1/2 tsp ground coriander
- 1/2 tsp ground turmeric
- 1/2 C. heavy whipping cream
- 1/2 tsp salt

- 1/2 bunch cilantro for garnish

Directions

- In a large bowl, add the yogurt, 2 tsp of the garam masala, paprika, black pepper, 1/2 tsp of the salt, cayenne pepper and 1/2 tsp of the coriander and mix till well combined.
- Add the chicken strips and coat with the mixture generously.
- Refrigerate, covered for about 2 hours.
- Set your oven to 450 degrees F and grease a baking sheet.
- Arrange the chicken strips onto the prepared baking sheet in a single layer.
- Cook in the oven for about 10 minutes.
- Remove from the oven and keep aside.
- In a large skillet, heat the vegetable oil on medium heat and sauté the cumin seeds for about 3 minutes.
- Add the onion and sauté for about 4-5 minutes.
- Stir in garlic, ginger, and green chilis and cook for about 15 to 20 minutes.
- Stir in the tomatoes, tomato paste and water and cook for about 10 minutes, stirring occasionally.
- Stir in 1 tsp of the garam masala, 1/2 tsp of the coriander, turmeric, cooked chicken and cream and simmer, covered for about 10 minutes.
- Season with 1/2 tsp of the salt and remove from the heat.
- Serve with a garnishing of the cilantro.

Amount per serving (4 total)

Timing Information:

Preparation	20 m
Cooking	55 m
Total Time	3 h 15 m

Nutritional Information:

Calories	403 kcal
Fat	25 g
Carbohydrates	20.5g
Protein	27.2 g
Cholesterol	100 mg
Sodium	927 mg

* Percent Daily Values are based on a 2,000 calorie diet.

Thai Entrée Chicken Curry

Ingredients

- 1 tbsp vegetable oil
- 1 tsp curry paste, see appendix
- 1 1/4 lb. skinless, boneless chicken breast meat - cut into strips
- 1 onion, coarsely chopped
- 1 red bell pepper, cut into strips
- 1 tbsp grated lemon zest
- 1 C. light coconut milk
- 1 tbsp fish sauce
- 1 tbsp fresh lemon juice
- 1/3 C. chopped fresh cilantro

Directions

- In a large skillet, heat the vegetable oil on medium heat and sauté the curry paste for about 30 seconds.
- Add the chicken and cook for about 3 minutes.
- Stir in the onion, bell pepper, lemon zest, coconut milk, fish sauce and lemon juice and bring to a boil.
- Cooked for about 5-7 minutes.
- Serve hot with the sprinkling of the cilantro.

Amount per serving (4 total)

Timing Information:

Preparation	25 m
Cooking	10 m
Total Time	35 m

Nutritional Information:

Calories	269 kcal
Fat	12.3 g
Carbohydrates	6.4g
Protein	30.9 g
Cholesterol	81 mg
Sodium	379 mg

* Percent Daily Values are based on a 2,000 calorie diet.

After Work Crock Pot Orange Curry

Ingredients

- 5 (6 oz.) boneless skinless chicken breasts
- salt and pepper, to taste
- 1 (12 oz.) jar orange marmalade
- 1/2 C. chicken stock
- 1 1/2 tsp curry powder
- 1/2 tsp ground cayenne pepper
- 1 pinch ground ginger

Directions

- Season the chicken breasts with the salt and pepper.
- In a bowl, add the marmalade, chicken stock, curry powder, cayenne pepper and ground ginger and beat till well combined.
- In a slow cooker, place the chicken breasts and top with the marmalade mixture evenly.
- Set the slow cooker on High and cook, covered for about 3-4 hours, flipping once in the middle way.

Amount per serving (5 total)

Timing Information:

Preparation	10 m
Cooking	3 h
Total Time	3 h 10 m

Nutritional Information:

Calories	342 kcal
Fat	3.6 g
Carbohydrates	45.3g
Protein	33.5 g
Cholesterol	88 mg
Sodium	179 mg

* Percent Daily Values are based on a 2,000 calorie diet.

Peanut Butter Coconut Curry

Ingredients

- 2 tbsp vegetable oil
- 3 tbsp curry paste, see appendix
- 1 (3/4 inch thick) slice ginger, minced
- 1 1/4 lb. skinless, boneless chicken breast meat - cubed
- 3 tbsp brown sugar
- 3 tbsp fish sauce
- 3 tbsp tamarind paste
- 1/3 C. peanut butter
- 3 C. peeled, cubed potatoes
- 1 (13.5 oz.) can coconut milk
- 3 tbsp fresh lime juice

Directions

- In a large pan, heat the vegetable oil on medium heat and sauté the curry paste and minced ginger for about 2 minutes.
- Stir in the chicken cubes and cook for about 3 minutes.
- Stir in the brown sugar, fish sauce, tamarind paste, peanut butter, potatoes and coconut milk and bring to a boil.
- Reduce the heat to medium-low and simmer, covered for about 20 minutes.
- Add the lime juice and cook for about 5 minutes.

Amount per serving (4 total)

Timing Information:

Preparation	20 m
Cooking	35 m
Total Time	55 m

Nutritional Information:

Calories	690 kcal
Fat	41.2 g
Carbohydrates	47.3g
Protein	38.1 g
Cholesterol	73 mg
Sodium	1221 mg

* Percent Daily Values are based on a 2,000 calorie diet.

4-Ingredient Alternative Curry

Ingredients

- 1 C. orange marmalade
- 1 tbsp curry powder
- 1 tsp salt
- 1/2 C. water
- 4 bone-in chicken breast halves, with skin

Directions

- Set your oven to 350 degrees F before doing anything else and lightly grease a 13x9-inch baking dish.
- In a small bowl, mix together the marmalade, curry powder, salt and water.
- Arrange the chicken breasts in the prepared baking dish, cut side down and top with the marmalade mixture evenly.
- Cook in the oven for about 45 minutes, spooning sauce over chicken occasionally. (If sauce begins to stick to the baking dish you can add about 1/4 C. of the water).
- Transfer the chicken into a plate.
- Skim off the fat from the top of the sauce.
- Serve the hot sauce with the chicken.

Amount per serving (4 total)

Timing Information:

Preparation	10 m
Cooking	1 h
Total Time	1 h 20 m

Nutritional Information:

Calories	589 kcal
Fat	21 g
Carbohydrates	54g
Protein	47.4 g
Cholesterol	144 mg
Sodium	769 mg

* Percent Daily Values are based on a 2,000 calorie diet.

Easy Guyanese Potato Curry

Ingredients

- 3 tbsp vegetable oil
- 1 (3 lb.) chicken, cut into pieces
- 1 large onion, diced
- 6 cloves garlic, minced
- 4 large potatoes - peeled and cubed
- 2 tbsp salt
- 1/4 C. Jamaican curry powder, see appendix
- hot pepper sauce to taste

Directions

- In a large pan, heat the oil on medium-high heat and cook the chicken, onions and garlic for about 5 minutes.
- Stir in the potatoes, salt, curry powder and enough water to cover the chicken halfway and simmer, covered for about 30-40 minutes.
- Stir in the hot pepper sauce and remove from the heat.

Amount per serving (8 total)

Timing Information:

Preparation	25 m
Cooking	35 m
Total Time	1 h

Nutritional Information:

Calories	574 kcal
Fat	31.4 g
Carbohydrates	36.6g
Protein	36.1 g
Cholesterol	128 mg
Sodium	1908 mg

* Percent Daily Values are based on a 2,000 calorie diet.

Jakarta Inspired Curry

Ingredients

- 1/2 C. coconut milk
- 1 tbsp red curry paste, see appendix
- 1 lb. skinless, boneless chicken breast, cut in bite-sized pieces
- 2 C. coconut milk
- 3 tbsp fish sauce
- 1 tbsp brown sugar
- 3/4 C. bamboo shoots, drained
- 2 C. frozen mixed vegetables, thawed
- 1/2 red bell pepper, sliced
- 1/2 orange bell pepper, sliced
- 3/4 C. fresh Thai basil leaves
- 2 tbsp fresh lime juice

Directions

- In a heavy pan, add 1/2 C. of the coconut milk and bring to a boil.
- Stir in the curry paste and cook for about 5 minutes.
- Add the chicken and cook for about 5 minutes.
- Stir in 2 C. of the coconut milk, fish sauce, sugar, vegetables, bamboo shoots and basil and simmer for about 15 minutes.

- Drizzle with the lime juice and remove from the heat.
- Serve warm.

Amount per serving (5 total)

Timing Information:

Preparation	20 m
Cooking	25 m
Total Time	45 m

Nutritional Information:

Calories	385 kcal
Fat	26.5 g
Carbohydrates	18.1g
Protein	23.3 g
Cholesterol	47 mg
Sodium	801 mg

* Percent Daily Values are based on a 2,000 calorie diet.

Fruit Curry II

Ingredients

- 1 tbsp butter
- 1 onion, chopped
- 3 cloves garlic, minced
- 2 lb. skinless, boneless chicken breast meat - cut into bite-size pieces
- 3 tbsp curry paste, see appendix
- 1/2 C. mango chutney, see appendix
- 1 (28 oz.) can diced tomatoes, drained

Directions

- In a large skillet, melt the butter on medium-high heat and sauté the onion and garlic for about 2-3 minutes.
- Add the chicken and sauté for about 30 seconds.
- Add the curry paste and stir to coat well.
- Add the chutney and tomatoes and cook for about 10 minutes.

Amount per serving (6 total)

Timing Information:

Preparation	15 m
Cooking	20 m
Total Time	35 m

Nutritional Information:

Calories	261 kcal
Fat	5.7 g
Carbohydrates	16.5g
Protein	33.1 g
Cholesterol	91 mg
Sodium	443 mg

* Percent Daily Values are based on a 2,000 calorie diet.

Burma Curry

Ingredients

- 1/4 C. vegetable oil
- 8 shallots, thinly sliced
- 1 lb. skinless, boneless chicken meat, cut into large pieces
- 2 tbsp red curry paste, see appendix
- 1 tbsp curry powder
- 1/2 C. coconut milk
- 1/4 C. pureed tomato
- 2 tbsp fish sauce
- 1 tbsp palm sugar
- 2 medium tomatoes, cut into wedges
- 1 bunch cilantro, chopped

Directions

- In a large skillet, heat the vegetable oil on low heat and sauté the shallots till tender.
- With a slotted spoon, transfer the shallots in a bowl and keep aside.
- In the same skillet, add the chicken, curry paste and curry powder and enough water to cover and bring to a boil.
- Reduce the heat to low and simmer, covered till the chicken is done completely.

- Stir in the coconut milk, tomato puree, fish sauce, palm sugar and 1/2 of the tomato wedges and simmer till the mixture becomes smooth and creamy.
- Stir in the remaining tomatoes and simmer till tender.
- Serve with a topping of the cilantro and fried shallots.

Amount per serving (4 total)

Timing Information:

Preparation	20 m
Cooking	30 m
Total Time	50 m

Nutritional Information:

Calories	425 kcal
Fat	23.7 g
Carbohydrates	26.5g
Protein	28.8 g
Cholesterol	79 mg
Sodium	806 mg

* Percent Daily Values are based on a 2,000 calorie diet.

Easy Malay Curry

Ingredients

- 1 tbsp vegetable oil
- 1/2 lb. skinless, boneless chicken breast, cubed
- 1/2 C. chicken stock
- 1 tbsp soy sauce
- 1 tbsp cider vinegar
- 1 1/2 tbsp brown sugar
- 1 tsp curry powder
- 1 tbsp cornstarch
- 1/2 onion, diced
- 1 green bell pepper, sliced
- 1 red bell pepper, sliced
- 2 tsp minced fresh ginger root
- 1 mango, peeled and cubed

Directions

- In a large skillet, heat the vegetable oil on medium-high heat and cook the chicken breast till browned completely.
- Transfer the chicken into a plate.
- Meanwhile in a bowl, add the chicken stock, soy sauce, vinegar, brown sugar, curry powder and cornstarch and beat till well combined.

- In the same skillet sauté the onion on medium heat for about 5 minutes.
- Stir in the green and red bell peppers and cook for about 2 minutes.
- Add the ginger and cook for about 1 minute.
- Stir in the chicken stock mixture and cooked chicken breast and cook till the sauce becomes thick.
- Stir in the mango and cook till heated completely.
- Serve hot.

Amount per serving (2 total)

Timing Information:

Preparation	20 m
Cooking	20 m
Total Time	40 m

Nutritional Information:

Calories	361 kcal
Fat	9.1 g
Carbohydrates	42g
Protein	29 g
Cholesterol	66 mg
Sodium	708 mg

* Percent Daily Values are based on a 2,000 calorie diet.

Thursday's Night Curry and Rice

Ingredients

- 1 tsp curry powder
- 1/2 tsp salt
- 1/4 tsp black pepper
- 4 skinless, boneless chicken breast halves
- 1 C. chicken broth
- 1/2 C. water
- 1/2 C. white wine
- 1 C. long-grain white rice
- 1 tbsp brown sugar
- 1 tbsp dried parsley
- 1 C. diced mango

Directions

- In a large bowl, mix together the curry powder, 1/4 tsp of the salt and pepper.
- Add the chicken breasts and rub with the mixture generously.
- In a large, non-stick skillet, add the chicken broth, water, wine, rice, brown sugar, dried parsley, remaining 1/4 tsp salt and mango and stir to combine.
- Place the chicken breasts over the rice mixture and bring to a boil.

- Reduce the heat to low and simmer, covered for about 20-25 minutes.
- Remove from the heat and keep aside, covered, for about 5 minutes.

Amount per serving (4 total)

Timing Information:

Preparation	15 m
Cooking	30 m
Total Time	45 m

Nutritional Information:

Calories	379 kcal
Fat	3 g
Carbohydrates	53.8g
Protein	27.1 g
Cholesterol	61 mg
Sodium	347 mg

* Percent Daily Values are based on a 2,000 calorie diet.

Canadian Inspired Curry

Ingredients

- 2 tbsp olive oil
- 2 tbsp butter
- 1 large onion, chopped
- 1 red bell pepper, seeded and chopped
- 1 yellow bell pepper, seeded and chopped
- 1 green bell pepper, seeded and chopped
- 2 C. cubed cooked chicken breast meat
- 3 cloves garlic
- 1 tsp sugar
- 1/4 C. pure maple syrup
- 1 C. heavy cream
- 2 1/2 tbsp hot curry paste, see appendix

Directions

- In a large pan, melt the butter on medium heat and sauté the onion and peppers till tender.
- Stir in the cooked chicken, garlic and sugar and cook for about 3 minutes, stirring continuously.
- Stir in the maple syrup and cook for about 5 minutes.
- Stir in the curry paste and heavy cream.
- Reduce the heat to low and simmer, uncovered for about 10-15 minutes.

Amount per serving (4 total)

Timing Information:

Preparation	5 m
Cooking	30 m
Total Time	35 m

Nutritional Information:

Calories	546 kcal
Fat	40 g
Carbohydrates	26.4g
Protein	21.9 g
Cholesterol	149 mg
Sodium	292 mg

* Percent Daily Values are based on a 2,000 calorie diet.

Appendix I: Spice Mixes, Curry Pastes, and Chutneys

Jamaican Curry Spice Mix

Not all curries come out of Asia. This Caribbean style curry will provide a new and unique taste this is characteristic of the islands.

Ingredients

- 1/4 C. whole coriander seeds
- 2 tbsps whole cumin seeds
- 2 tbsps whole mustard seeds
- 2 tbsps whole anise seeds
- 1 tbsp whole fenugreek seeds
- 1 tbsp whole allspice berries
- 5 tbsps ground turmeric

Directions

- Combine the coriander seeds, cumin seeds, mustard seeds, anise seeds, fenugreek seeds, and allspice berries in a skillet.
- Toast over medium heat until the color of the spices slightly darkens, and the spices are very fragrant, about 10 minutes. Remove the spices from the skillet, and allow

them to cool to room temperature. Grind the spices with the turmeric in a spice grinder. Store in an airtight container at room temperature.
- Get a frying hot without oil, toast the following for 11 mins: allspice berries, coriander seeds, fenugreek seeds, cumin seeds, anise seeds, and mustard seeds.
- Get a mortar and pestle or your preferred grinder and grind all the toasted spices with turmeric as well.
- Enter everything into your storage containers.

Timing Information:

Preparation	Cooking	Total Time
10 m	11 m	21 m

Nutritional Information:

Calories	12 kcal
Fat	0.5 g
Carbohydrates	1.8g
Protein	0.5 g
Cholesterol	0 mg
Sodium	2 mg

* Percent Daily Values are based on a 2,000 calorie diet.

Garam Masala Spice Mix

This version of the masala spice mix is inspired by Pakistan. You can play with the seasonings a bit if it is too spicy. But spicy the spiciness is intended.

Ingredients

- 1/4 C. black cumin seed
- 2 large bay leaves, crushed
- 2 tbsps green cardamom seeds
- 1/4 C. black peppercorns
- 1 1/2 tsps whole cloves
- 1 tbsp fennel seed
- 1 tsp chopped fresh mace
- 4 cinnamon sticks, broken
- 1 pinch ground nutmeg

Directions

- Toast the following in a skillet for 11 mins: cinnamon sticks, cumin, mace, bay leaves. Fennel seed, cardamom, cloves, and peppercorns.
- With your grinder or mortar and pestle process the spices into a fine powder and store in your favorite container.

Timing Information:

Preparation	Cooking	Total Time
5 m		5 m

Nutritional Information:

Calories	24 kcal
Fat	0.7 g
Carbohydrates	4.1g
Protein	0.8 g
Cholesterol	0 mg
Sodium	6 mg

* Percent Daily Values are based on a 2,000 calorie diet.

Classical Indian Curry Paste

Ingredients
- 2 1/2 tbsps coriander seeds, ground
- 1 tbsp cumin seed, ground
- 1 tsp brown mustard seeds
- 1/2 tsp cracked black peppercorns
- 1 tsp chili powder
- 1 tsp ground turmeric
- 2 crushed garlic cloves
- 2 tsps grated fresh ginger
- 3-4 tbsps white vinegar

Directions
- Get a bowl, combine: coriander seeds, cumin seeds, mustard seeds, black peppercorns, chili powder, turmeric, cloves, and ginger. Stir the mix completely and evenly. Combine in the vinegar and begin to mash everything together into a paste.
- Place your paste into a jar and seal the lid tightly. Your paste will stay fresh in the fridge for about 3 to 4 weeks.
- Enjoy.

Servings per Recipe: 1

Timing Information:

Preparation	5 mins
Total Time	5 mins

Nutritional Information:

Calories	225.4
Fat	10.4 g
Cholesterol	0 mg
Sodium	91 mg
Carbohydrates	33.3 g
Protein	8.8 g

* Percent Daily Values are based on a 2,000 calorie diet.

Simple Homemade Red Curry Paste (Thailand Style)

To prepare a red curry paste use red chilies for a green curry paste use green chilies.

Ingredients
- ¼ C. chopped scallion
- ¼ C. chopped fresh cilantro
- 2 tbsps minced garlic
- 2 tbsps grated fresh gingerroot
- 1 tbsp freshly grated lemon rinds
- 1 tbsp brown sugar
- 1-2 fresh red chilies or 1-2 green chili, minced
- 3 tbsps fresh lemon juice
- 1 tbsp ground coriander
- 1 tsp turmeric
- ½ tsp salt

Directions
- Add the following your food processor: scallion, cilantro, garlic, ginger root, lemons / lime, brown sugar, chilies, lemon / lime juice, coriander, turmeric, and salt.
- Process and pulse everything until it becomes a smooth paste.
- Enjoy.

Servings per Recipe: 1

Timing Information:

Preparation	10 mins
Total Time	10 mins

Nutritional Information:

Calories	300.4
Fat	3.5 g
Cholesterol	0 mg
Sodium	2368.8 mg
Carbohydrates	71.1 g
Protein	7.5 g

* Percent Daily Values are based on a 2,000 calorie diet.

Mango Chutney I

Ingredients

- 2 lb. very firm mango
- 2 C. sugar
- 1.5 C. vinegar
- 1 (5 cm) pieces ginger, peeled
- 4 cloves garlic, peeled
- 2 -4 tsps chili powder
- 4 tsps mustard seeds
- 8 tsps salt
- 1 C. raisins

Directions

- Peel the mango and then remove the pit and chop it.
- In a pan, add sugar and vinegar, leaving about 20ml and simmer, stirring occasionally for about 10 minutes.
- Meanwhile in a food processor, add remaining vinegar, garlic and ginger and pulse till a paste forms.
- Transfer the paste into a pan and simmer, stirring continuously for about 10 minutes.
- Stir in the mango and remaining ingredients and simmer, stirring occasionally for about 25 minutes or till desired thickness of chutney.

- Transfer the chutney into hot sterilized jars and seal tightly and keep aside to cool.
- This chutney can be stored in dark place for about 1 year but remember to refrigerate after opening.

Amount per serving: 1

Timing Information:

Preparation	20 mins
Total Time	1 hr 5 mins

Nutritional Information:

Calories	627.2
Fat	2.1g
Cholesterol	0.0mg
Sodium	3748.7mg
Carbohydrates	153.4g
Protein	4.2g

* Percent Daily Values are based on a 2,000 calorie diet.

Mango Chutney II

Ingredients

- 4 medium mangoes, peeled and coarsely chopped (1.7kg)
- 3/4 C. port wine, optional
- 2 large white onions, chopped finely (400g)
- 1 C. coarsely chopped raisins (170g)
- 2 tsps grated fresh ginger
- 2 fresh Thai red chili peppers, chopped finely
- 2 C. sugar (440g)
- 3 C. malt vinegar
- 2 tsps yellow mustard seeds

Directions

- In a large heavy-bottomed pan, add all the ingredients and simmer, stirring continuously till the sugar dissolves.
- Simmer, stirring occasionally for about 90 minutes or till desired thickness of chutney.
- Transfer the chutney into hot sterilized jars and seal tightly and keep aside to cool.
- This chutney can be stored in dark place for about 6 months but remember to refrigerate after opening.

Amount per serving: 1

Timing Information:

Preparation	20 mins
Total Time	1 hr 50 mins

Nutritional Information:

Calories	612.4
Fat	1.0g
Cholesterol	0.0mg
Sodium	16.2mg
Carbohydrates	144.7g
Protein	3.0g

* Percent Daily Values are based on a 2,000 calorie diet.

CURRIED APRICOT CHUTNEY

Ingredients

- 1 medium onion, chopped
- 1 inch piece gingerroot, peeled and minced
- 2 C. drained canned apricots
- 1/2 C. white sugar or 1/2 C. brown sugar
- 1 C. apple cider or 1 C. rice wine vinegar
- 3 C. water
- 1 tsp curry powder
- 4 cardamom pods
- 2 inches cinnamon sticks
- minced chili pepper (optional)

Directions

- In a pan, mix together all the ingredients and bring to a boil.
- Reduce the heat to low and simmer, stirring occasionally for about 90 minutes or till desired thickness of chutney.

Amount per serving: 1

Timing Information:

| Preparation | 15 mins |
| Total Time | 1 hr 15 mins |

Nutritional Information:

Calories	758.4
Fat	0.6g
Cholesterol	0.0mg
Sodium	38.8mg
Carbohydrates	195.7g
Protein	3.9g

* Percent Daily Values are based on a 2,000 calorie diet.

THANKS FOR READING! JOIN THE CLUB AND KEEP ON COOKING WITH 6 MORE COOKBOOKS....

http://bit.ly/1TdrStv

To grab the box sets simply follow the link mentioned above, or tap one of book covers.

This will take you to a page where you can simply enter your email address and a PDF version of the box sets will be emailed to you.

Hope you are ready for some serious cooking!

http://bit.ly/1TdrStv

COME ON...
LET'S BE FRIENDS :)

We adore our readers and love connecting with them socially.

Like BookSumo on Facebook and let's get social!

Facebook

And also check out the BookSumo Cooking Blog.

Food Lover Blog

Printed in Great Britain
by Amazon